An American Postal Portrait

A Photographic Legacy

UNITED STATES POSTAL SERVICE

HarperResource

A Division of HarperCollins*Publishers*

ACKNOWLEDGMENTS

This book was produced by the United States Postal Service.

William J. Henderson, Postmaster General and Chief Executive Officer

Deborah K. Willhite, Senior Vice President, Government Relations and Public Policy

Azeezaly S. Jaffer, Vice President, Public Affairs and Communications

James C. Tolbert, Jr., Executive Director, Stamp Services

SPECIAL THANKS ARE EXTENDED TO THE FOLLOWING INDIVIDUALS FOR THEIR CONTRIBUTIONS:

Patrick McCabe, U.S. Postal Service, Editor/Photography Editor

Terry McCaffrey, U.S. Postal Service, Designer/Photography Editor

Carl Burcham, U.S. Postal Service, Writer

Roberta Wojtkowski, Art Production

Michael Lilly, U.S. Postal Service, Assistant Editor/Researcher

Ellen Plummer, Photo Researcher

Rebecca Hirsh, Hunter Hoffman, PhotoAssist Inc., Photo Researchers

Rita Moroney, U.S. Postal Service, Historian (Emeritus)

Megaera Ausman, U.S. Postal Service, Historian

Gerald Merna, Kelley Sullivan, Dan Afzal, U.S. Postal Service, Photo Production

Kelly Spinks, U.S. Postal Service, Project Manager

Megan Newman, HarperResource, Editorial Director

Greg Chaput, HarperResource, Associate Editor

Lucy Albanese, HarperCollins General Books Group, Design Director

Roberto de Vicq de Cumptich, HarperResource, Art Director

Library of Congress Card Number: 98-60904

An American Postal Portrait:/U.S. Postal Service

First Edition

ISBN: 0-06-019900-8

Dedication

Dedicated to the proud men and women
of the United States Postal Service
and their predecessors for more than two centuries
of dedication and commitment to quality service.

Above: *Two New Jersey youngsters in the 1920s stretch to reach one of the small letter boxes commonplace to America's sidewalks.* **Front Cover:** *1926 letter carrier, Genevieve Baskfield of Zumbrota, Minnesota.* **Endpapers:** *1905 Boston letter carriers brass band.* **Back Cover:** *In 1893, San Antonio letter carrier Henry Schmidt sits in his one-horse carriage, the first of its kind to be used for mail delivery in the city.*

Contents

Foreword

William J. Henderson

Postmaster General

and Chief Executive Officer

We await its arrival with anticipation. We listen for the footsteps nearing the door. We hear the hinge squeak. We see the light streaming through the aperture. We wait, expectantly, watching and listening for the completion of the journey. The pot on the stove goes unstirred. The telephone goes unanswered. The latest must-see television program goes unwatched. ■ The mail has arrived. ■ It is the mail's powerful connection with the American people that we celebrate in these pages. *An American Postal Portrait* is a photographic legacy of the United States Postal Service. Beginning with the advent of photography in the 1860s to the present, these pages portray the people, places and events that have shaped the Postal Service and at the same time touched all American lives. ■ The diversity of our workforce, our innovative technology and our unique imprint on American life are recorded in photographs compiled from the collections of the United States Postal Service, National Archives, Library of Congress and other sources. Included are the works of postal photographers and others, such as the influential Walker Evans, who helped develop American documentary photography in the 1930s. ■ These photographs are a testament to the influential role the women and men who deliver the mail have played in shaping the decades. These images portray a Postal Service that has marched stride by stride with America into the future, from its rural, isolated beginnings to its high-tech, information-driven present. ■ These faces are America's faces. These places are America's places. This is more than just a portrait of the Postal Service. This is a scrapbook from the American experience. ■ Linger over these images. Imagine the lives we've all led. Stagecoach drivers. Pioneers of flight. Exploration – and a postal clerk! – at the South Pole. As the nation expanded, so did we. As technology advanced, so did we. ■ Like the age-old question of which came first, the chicken or the egg, the question could be asked, which came first, Rural Free Delivery or rural roads? Without a doubt, the reach of mail delivery into even the most isolated hamlets connected people with each other like never before. ■ Did you know Charles Lindbergh was a postal pilot, and that we helped develop the airline industry? ■ While these photographs recall times past, they speak also to the future. The Postal Service will continue to play an important role in shaping the future of our nation. We will continue to meet the challenge of providing universal mail service to all Americans. This is our legacy. ■ As an amateur photographer, I respect the power of the camera to capture memories, to entertain and surprise, to provoke thought and to reveal truth. This collection of photographs captures the essence of Postal Service life. ■ Linger over the images. Imagine the lives we've *all* led. ■ While the future portrait of the Postal Service has yet to be taken – and it likely will involve a digital camera – the journey so far has been remarkable. ■ Amazing how time flies… like an eagle. ■ Welcome to our family album.

Right: Since the late 19th century, rural mailboxes like this one have connected rural America to other parts of the country and the outside world.

Introduction

James L. Bruns

Director, National Postal Museum

Smithsonian Institution

America's postal system, which so many of our citizens take for granted today, is a truly remarkable democratic achievement. Since the founding of our republic, our Postal Service has strived to serve the universal needs of all Americans. It has done this by maintaining an efficient, inexpensive and trustworthy means of exchanging personal and business communications. ■ From its start, the Postal Service mission has been to ensure that our nation receives the best possible service. But even more important, our postal system has helped to bind our growing nation together. This latter point was an essential mandate, for, as George Washington predicted, the postal system would be the principal means by which the people of the United States would be bound together in loyalty to the government. ■ The movement of the mails has played a significant part in the growth of our country. It has followed closely upon the footsteps of prospectors and homesteaders. Whenever a mining camp or small community was formed, a rush of people would typically follow, mail service would be created, and a post office would be established. This pattern of growth ensured the prompt distribution of the latest news to our ever-expanding population. And this remains true today. Indeed, it does not matter where one lives—whether in an affluent suburb or the inner city, whether in northern Alaska or at the bottom of the Grand Canyon—every American receives mail! ■ The arrival of the mail has always been one of life's great pleasures. We look forward to discovering what is in the mail for us. This anticipation has not changed in more than 200 years. In earlier generations, work stopped and church services occasionally ended early when the mail arrived. ■ The mail that is, and has been, carried by the dedicated employees of the United States Postal Service has helped to shape the character and quality of life of every American every delivery day. Because Americans from all walks of life, from all corners of the country and from diverse ancestry send and receive mail, we share a common experience. The impact of that shared experience reveals itself differently to each of us every delivery day. To an elderly American, it may be demonstrated by the arrival of a loving missive from a distant friend or family member, along with a well-earned Social Security or retirement check. For those raised on a farm or residing in one of the country's many rural hamlets, it may be reflected by the arrival of some recently ordered merchandise from across the world. Or, for an anxious high school student anywhere in America, it may come in the form of an acceptance letter to a college or university, or a highly prized job offer. ■ Delivering letters is not the only thing the Postal Service has done for America over the years. Since the 1850s, it has been called upon to provide a variety of public services that have little to do with mail delivery. It has distributed over a million pounds of free vegetable and flower seeds at Congress's request, distributed tax forms, assisted in hog surveys and draft and Selective Service registrations, sold Federal Duck Stamps to waterfowl hunters, coordinated the gathering of weather forecasting information, assisted in

registering aliens, sold savings bonds, served as banks in many small communities as part of the nation's postal savings system and furnished flags for the burial of veterans. Over the years our nation's postal employees have provided such additional services without question of compensation. ■ The United States Postal Service is business at its best. While the United States occupies only about 1/50th of the land surface of the globe, our postal system handles approximately 41 percent of the world's mail volume—650 million pieces every day, 3.9 billion pieces every week. The next largest country is Japan, with 6 percent of the world's mail volume. To serve the American people, the Postal Service places 2.7 billion pounds of mail aboard approximately 15,000 commercial airline flights annually. So much of America's mail goes by air that the Postal Service is the airlines' biggest shipper; but postal people do more than that. As part of our service, our postal employees deliver 24 pieces of mail to more than 130 million households and businesses every week. Our postal employees collect mail from 312,000 curbside mail collection boxes each day, place mail in more than 18 million post office lockboxes for customers desiring that service, and process 38 million address changes each year to ensure prompt and reliable service. Our postal employees take care of America's mailers every day everywhere. ■ But perhaps most important of all, the United States Postal Service also gives substance to the American ideal of freedom of expression. The recognition of the vital importance of this freedom was one of the great triumphs of the American Revolution. Our right to speak freely is not confined

to oral expression. To be meaningful, freedom of speech must be freely translated into our letters, books, newspapers and magazines, and all other mailable materials. That was so apparent to the writers of the Constitution that they insisted upon both a postal system and a free press. The Congress went even further in 1792 with the enactment of the Post Office Act, which among other things called for the expansion of post roads, the sanctity of the mails and the inclusion of general publications. In effect, the Act subsidized the free press. It established cheap newspaper rates. Magazines and pamphlets were charged slightly more than newspapers, but much less than letters. These price breaks were an incentive to the distribution of news. It was a small price to pay for national unity. The circulation of such publications was seen as "the strongest bulwark of free government." Attempts to curb their exchange were envisioned as an "unconstitutional means of stopping in any degree the sources of that information which distinguishes America from the people of all other countries." This right to communicate freely with one another—to express our ideas without fear of censorship—is the priceless heritage of a free society. It also is a distinguishing characteristic of our American way of life. Truly, the sanctity of the mails is a basic freedom without which all of our other freedoms would be in jeopardy. ■ Because the Postal Service belongs to the people whom it serves, these pages represent an American scrapbook. These historic images portray the dedication, and achievement of America's postal employees. These pages form a truly American postal portrait.

Above: *RFD carriers, such as this one outside Milwaukee, Wisconsin,*

became a primary link for rural residents to the outside world.

1860-1900

The Formative Years

During the 19th century, America experienced a dynamic social, cultural and geographical metamorphosis from former British colony to the world's largest and most powerful country. The key events that shaped the era—Civil War, westward expansion and the Industrial Revolution—forever altered the face of the nation and its postal system. ■ In 1800, only a handful of post offices dotted the eastern seaboard. By 1863, nearly 30,000 post offices operated in large and small communities nationwide, and by the turn of the century that figure had swelled to 77,000. Postal revenues skyrocketed as well, from $11 million in 1864 to more than $100 million by 1900. ■ Responding to the urgent need for prompter and more reliable mail service, visionary Postmasters General such as Montgomery Blair (1861–1864) and John Wanamaker (1889–1893) introduced innovations that would have lasting impact on the American postal system, such as the uniform letter rate (1863), free city delivery (1863), railway post office (1864), special delivery service (1885), rural free delivery (1891) and the pneumatic tube system (1893). ■ The road to reform was difficult, plagued by seemingly insurmountable obstacles such as the Civil War. For four grueling years (1861–1865), the bloody conflict divided the nation and the postal system. Mail exchange between North and South was discontinued and replaced by separate Union and Confederate post offices. ■ Despite the division, postal service was amazingly reliable. Postmaster General William Dennison noted in his 1864 Annual Report: "(Union Army) soldiers receive

their mail with as much regularity and promptness as is possible for armies in the field, and with as much certainty and security as the most favored patrons of the country." ■ Natural catastrophes threatened the mail system as well. But in the aftermath of every disaster, postal employees responded with characteristic fervor and dedication. The Chicago fire of 1871 destroyed 17,000 buildings, but carriers were back on the street even as the embers continued to glow. The Johnstown flood of 1889 killed 2,200 people and devastated Pennsylvania's Conemagh Valley, yet mail service was back to normal within several days. ■ When the Post Office Department was not *restoring* mail service, it was *extending* it to new customers via rural free delivery (RFD). RFD linked isolated residents to the outside world, stimulated commerce and encouraged road improvements. Just five years after the 1896 full-scale introduction of RFD, Postmaster General Charles Emory Smith reported that the service was "the most salient, significant and far-reaching feature of postal development in recent times." ■ While RFD was making its mark in the East, mail carriers and postal contractors were enduring outlaw and Indian attacks, disease and drought to move the mail in the West. Western roads were muddy, dusty and always treacherous. Operating from makeshift offices and general stores, western postmasters kept weapons nearby in case of robbery—a common occurrence. But the mail went through, thanks to dedicated postal employees who literally risked their lives to deliver the dreams and hopes of an expanding nation.

This carrier in 1895 was
authorized to wear a helmet,
much like the police helmet of
the day. The regulations also
required carriers to wear
badges while on duty.

Above: A Union Army mail wagon during the Civil War. Despite muddy, nearly impassable roads and extremes in temperature, wagon drivers maintained an exceptional record for efficiency. The "traveling post office" sold stamps and collected and distributed correspondence. **Left:** During the Civil War, a post office was established at the Army of the Potomac Headquarters in Falmouth, Virginia. Managed by Army Postmaster William B. Haslett, the postal system handled a daily volume of some 45,000 letters posted by and to Union soldiers in the field.

Above: *The huge influx of prospectors and others into Alaska during the Gold Rush of the 1890s caused the post office to dramatically increase service in the rugged and isolated territory. This Postal Inspector was dispatched in 1898 to oversee the performance of mail contractors.* **Left:** *As the Civil War came to a close in 1865, Milwaukee's 24 city letter carriers paused for a group photograph. Official letter carrier uniforms were first authorized about three years later in 1868.*

Above: During the great land rush to settle the Oklahoma Territory in 1889, the Oklahoma City Post Office was a converted chicken coop. From the makeshift building, Postmaster George A. Beidler, right, provided postal service to the thousands of homesteaders who had acquired inexpensive land tracts in this former Indian territory. Beidler's son Chase is shown toting a rifle. **Right:** Boston's French Empire–style post office, depicted here in 1900, is typical of the architecturally significant buildings erected by the Treasury Department for the Post Office Department until 1933.

Above: *One of Cedar Falls, Iowa's first city carriers was Ishmail Durrand Corning, shown here, circa 1898, in a photo along with son Duane posed in a mail satchel.* ***Right:*** *Between 1871 and 1887, the mail packet Chesapeake transported passengers, cargo, parcels and mail along the inland waterways of a rapidly expanding nation. Postal steamboats were so common that in 1823 Congress passed a law making steamboat routes "Post Roads" subject to federal regulation.*

Above: The use of bicycles for mail delivery, such as the one shown here in Salem,

Oregon, in 1888, became increasingly widespread during the 1890s.

Left: Stagecoaches, such as the one shown here leaving San Francisco in 1894,

carried passengers, cargo and mail through the West's rugged terrain. Heavily

armed coach drivers battled outlaws and dust storms to ensure the "certainty,

celerity and security" of the mails.

Far Left: *The first countywide rural free delivery service was established in 1899 from the Westminster (Carroll County), Maryland, Post Office. A driver and clerk/carrier operated the two-horse wagons, stopping to sell stamps, issue money orders, deliver mail and cancel stamps on collected letters. One-carrier routes replaced two-person service in 1905.*

Left, top & bottom: *No dog ever meant more to postal employees than Owney, the mascot of the Railway Mail Service. Befriended by workers at the Albany, New York, Post Office, Owney soon became fascinated by mailbags and traveling aboard Railway Post Offices. As his reputation grew, railway clerks and others began adding tags to his specially made vest commemorating each of the canine's visits. When he died in 1897, Owney had traveled more than 145,000 miles in 48 states, Mexico, Canada, China and Japan, receiving more than 1,000 tags and medals along the way. He is now stuffed and currently on exhibition at the National Postal Museum in Washington, DC.*

Above: *In the 1890s, dog sleds helped couriers provide mail service around Lake Superior's rugged north shore. In hazardous weather, especially in Alaska, contract carriers and their sled dogs braved frigid temperatures, sometimes reaching minus 60 degrees, to carry the mail. One route above the Arctic Circle was so demanding that the dogs were fitted with moccasins to protect their feet from the cold and ice, and they wore out 1,400 moccasins every year. The last sled-dog route operated in Alaska until 1963, when it was replaced by an airplane.* **Left:** *Letter carrier with two children on his route in St. Paul, Minnesota, 1890.*

Above: *As Postmaster General under Abraham Lincoln,*
Montgomery Blair initiated such dramatic postal innovations as free
city delivery, postal money orders and the Railway Post Office.
Blair's proposal to bring uniformity to international mail systems
resulted in the establishment of the Universal Postal Union, which has
become a model of international cooperation.

Left: In the 1830s, Alexis Clermont
carried mail on foot between
Green Bay and Chicago. In 1893,
during the Chicago World's Fair,
he retraced the 240-mile route.
Clermont was 85 at the time.

Above and right: Resembling a postal "chorus line," St. Louis' special delivery

messengers prepare to mount their bicycles for the day's work. Postal regulations of 1893

required that "none but reputable, active and intelligent boys should be employed

(as special delivery messengers), and they should in no case be under 13 years of age."

Above: Dapperly dressed postal employees take a break
for a photo in 1894 at the Hyde Park, Illinois, Post Office.

Left: Wearing a man's hat and shoes, the good-hearted Mary Fields was the second woman in America to regularly drive a mail stage. She poses here in front of the Mint Bar in Cascade, Montana, around 1900.

1901-1917

Visions of Grandeur

As the 20th century dawned, Americans were imbued with a compelling sense that anything was possible. Under the spirited Teddy Roosevelt and other ambitious leaders, every facet of American life underwent reform, including banking, labor, government . . . and the postal system. ■ Always eager to incorporate the latest technologies into daily operations, the Post Office Department began its continuing love affair with the century's two greatest modes of transportation—the automobile and the airplane. ■ In an age when horse and buggy were the norm, moving mail by the newfangled "horseless carriage" seemed an improbable and costly venture. But, with mail volume growing by leaps and bounds, local postmasters were in dire need of faster transportation. In 1906, they found it. That year, the Baltimore Post Office awarded a contract for two Columbia Mark 43 motor trucks to collect street-box letter mail. Contracted chauffeurs drove the vehicles, and postal employees collected the mail. ■ Within three years, postmasters of Milwaukee, Detroit, Washington, Indianapolis and Boston had purchased their own automotive fleets, and with the advent of Parcel Post in 1913, postmasters were experimenting with a wide variety of different types and styles of motorized vehicles. ■ Of all the methods of transportation tested between 1901 and 1917, however, none had a more dramatic effect on postal operations than the airplane. Though the federal government greeted aviation initiatives with skepticism, the Post Office Department embraced the idea of moving mail through the sky. ■ In 1911, pilot Earle Ovington crammed a mail pouch in the cockpit of his Bleriot monoplane and transported it seven miles to inaugurate American airmail service. The next year, Postmaster General Franklin Hitchcock noted: "There is reason to believe that in due course (airplanes) will be so far perfected as to render them an important agency in the transportation of mail." ■ Perhaps even greater postal progress would have been made if not for the outbreak of World War I. Railroads, then the primary means for moving passengers and mail, were seriously hampered by personnel shortages, as were post offices. Because of the number of male postal employees who had entered military service, post offices recruited women to deliver the mail. At the rate of 35 cents an hour — the same pay as men — they delivered the mail eight hours a day, six days a week. ■ Post offices played an important role in the war effort by providing a number of nonpostal services. Postmasters registered enemy aliens, handled paperwork for the draft and sold Liberty bonds and war savings certificates (more than 540 million in 1917 alone). Every post office became an employment agency for wartime industries, and small-town postmasters became recruiting officers. ■ For Americans and postal employees, the era that had begun with a sense of invulnerability and visions of grandeur had ended with a large dose of reality. Although the "war to end all wars" temporarily halted "normal, everyday life," it did not diminish dreams for a brighter future — especially for the men and women of the nation's postal service.

Right: By 1915, western cities such as Colorado Springs had begun to rely on automobiles for rural delivery.

Left: *A dapper Milwaukee postal employee poses for a photograph in 1907.* **Above:** *Regardless of the Deep South's subtropical humidity and sweltering temperatures, letter carriers of the early 1900s completed their appointed rounds in full dress flannel uniform.*

Above: In the early days of rural free delivery, the mailboxes erected by rural residents ranged from empty coal oil cans to lard pails hung on the fence. In 1902, the Post Office Department established rural mailbox standards for size, shape and accessibility and required stenciling with the phrase, "Approved by the Postmaster General." **Right:** San Francisco's 1906 earthquake and fires that followed greatly damaged the city's post office. By fighting fires, a handful of local employees saved the building from total destruction and the amount of mail lost was minor. Within two days, regular mail operations had begun again.

Above: "The Most Perfect and Convenient Wagons and Carts in Use for the Mail Collection Service" were manufactured by the Studebaker Brothers in South Bend, Indiana. Constructed to have practically no horse motion, wagons such as this model offered doors front and rear, a front seat with cushion, and one sliding window. **Right:** When this group photo was taken in 1906, free city delivery had been in existence in Evanston, Illinois, for almost 20 years. Undoubtedly, the post office's most renowned employee was Nathan Branch (center, front row), a runaway Kentucky slave and Civil War veteran who served as a special delivery messenger for several decades.

Left: *In 1900, a strong back and accurate throwing ability were good qualifications*

for employment in the New York Post Office Parcel Post section. **Above:** *Gold miners*

living in log cabins scattered around Eldora, Colorado, relied on the local post office

for provisions, banking and mail. The post office served this off-the-beaten-path

community for 70 years, from 1897 until 1967.

Left: *After delivering mail up and down the streets of Boston in 1905, the city's letter carriers formed a mostly brass band. Perhaps they played "The Postal March and Two-Step," composed by M. Vogt in 1902, or "The Postman's Song," by Ella Sterling Cummins and Saidee M.B. Larned.* **Above:** *During the 25th-anniversary celebration of this Cincinnati Post Office building in 1910, postal officials draped a five-story, 46-star American flag over the main facade and exhibited the pride of the Post Office Department, a railway post office car.*

Above: The Post Office Department began experimenting with the "horseless wagon" as early as 1896. Eleven years later, Milwaukee became one of the first cities in the nation to motorize the mails. These Johnson steam cars were innovations for their day, employing no crank or radiator. After testing cars and trucks in various cities under contract for several years, the Post Office Department established its own government-owned vehicle service in 1914. *Right:* New York City carriers proudly pose beside their fleet of mail trucks. The famous inscription over the post office reads: "Neither snow nor rain nor heat nor gloom of night stays these couriers from the swift completion of their appointed rounds." This quote is attributed to the ancient Greek historian Herodotus (circa 500 BC), who was describing the fidelity of Persian postal carriers.

Left: *Theophilus B. Travis began delivering the mail in Evanston, Illinois, in the mid-1890s and worked as a carrier until 1911. The larger collection boxes on today's streets were introduced in the 1890s and have gradually replaced the smaller, post-mounted receptacle shown in this photograph.* **Above:** *During the early years of Parcel Post, the Baltimore Post Office relied on White Motortrucks. In this 1914 photo, the individuals on duty were carriers Fred Helmer and Stewart Parks, along with driver James Morton.*

Above: Postmaster Sam Tapping (right) poses in front of the Fairhaven, Washington, Post Office with his three female clerks. *Right:* In another example of the long history of post offices serving all communities everywhere, Native Americans pose in front of Ruidoso Store and Post Office, Fort Stanton, New Mexico.

Above: *Airmail Pilot Earle Ovington.* **Left:** *In 1911, pilot Earle Ovington completed the first authorized airmail flight when he placed a bag of mail on his lap and flew his Bleriot monoplane seven miles from Garden City Estates to Mineola, New York. As planned, Ovington did not land. Instead, from an altitude of 200 feet he threw the mailbag from the plane. Unfortunately, the bag ripped in several places and Ovington watched Mineola's postmaster frantically chasing down 2,000 flying cards and letters.*

Above: Early Parcel Post light wagons were standard in length (6' 6"), height (6' 4") and look (green with red running boards, black striping and gold lettering). Heavy wagons were 18" longer, but otherwise were the same as light wagons. Among the cargo being loaded in this 1914 photograph are several automobile tires, a harbinger that spelled the ultimate demise of the horse-drawn wagon.

Left: On June 14, 1913, the Department celebrated its sixth annual observance of Flag Day at postal headquarters in Washington, DC. The ceremonies were highlighted by the unfurling of a mammoth "Old Glory," one of the world's largest at the time. Also on display in the courtyard were numerous smaller American flags and the Department's collection of state flags.

Left: Between 1895 and 1915, Boston's 15-trolley mail car system was the most elaborate of its kind in the nation. In this 1907 photo, employees transfer mail from trolley car #410 to mail wagon #18 in front of the Central Post Office. The last streetcar railway post offices operated in Baltimore until 1929. **Above:** Clerk Mary Stevens and Postmaster Edwin Holmes in the Detroit Lakes, Minnesota, Post Office in 1900. By 1906, nearly 28,000 women were employed in first- and second-class post offices alone.

Above: "Don't Call on Sunday" reads the hand-lettered sign on the Searsburg, Vermont, Post Office in this 1914 photograph. Postmaster Needham D. Bartlett is shown with Bible in hand. **Right:** Rural free delivery carrier, York County, Maine, 1930.

Above: The Post Office Department contracted out its motor vehicles until 1914, when the first official postal fleet was established. The early fleet was composed of a multitude of different vehicles of every shape and size. **Right:** In 1910, Lillie M. Donohoe served rural customers in Edgemoor, Delaware, from her horse-drawn mail vehicle.

Above: In 1919, Army post offices (APOs) overseas greatly resembled the small, rural post offices back in the states. Here, American servicemen sort mail at Army Post Office #785 in Allerey, Saone et Loire, France. During World War I and later wars, soldiers were given free mailing privileges. **Right:** In 1917, with many men serving in World War I, women entered all areas of the work force—including the city carrier forces of the post office. Mrs. Josephine Norton is shown here in New York City.

1918-1930

Flying High

The period following World War I was an era of experimentation tempered by tragedy. Having experienced four grueling years of hardship, Americans were eager to return to normal lives. During a frivolous time known as the "Roaring '20s," sports heroes Jack Dempsey, Babe Ruth and Bobby Jones made their mark; women exercised their newly earned right to vote; and motion pictures "learned to talk." Speakeasies, bumper seats, flappers and jazz were all the rage. There was a "chicken in every pot" and a job for all who chose to work. ■ During this period, the Post Office Department continued to pioneer airmail flight. In 1918, with a budget of little more than $100,000, the Aerial Mail Service flew more than 50,000 miles to transport 70,000 pounds of mail. By 1930, the Air Mail Service budget had grown to $15 million, and postal pilots were logging more than 15 million miles to carry 8 million pounds of mail. ■ Few American businesses had expressed interest in the possibilities of air travel during the early years of airmail service, but gradually commercial enterprises became intrigued by the possibility of moving passengers along with mail and cargo. As airmail service grew, so did commercial aviation; one service relied upon the other. ■ Early airmail pilots flew open-cockpit biplanes through snowstorms, thunderstorms, fog and high winds without the aid of instrumentation or assistance from ground personnel. Generally, their only navigational aids were the map they strapped to their legs and a half-full whiskey bottle rigged as a level indicator. The average lifespan for early pilots—900 hours flight time—reflected the dangers of the job. Between 1918 and 1930, 63 pilots died in flight. ■ But these early pilots were a determined and spirited group of daredevils, well aware of the dangers facing them. Pilot Jack Knight epitomized this group of daredevils as a member of the team that completed the first transcontinental day–night airmail flight. Taking off by the light of bonfires, Knight battled darkness, fog and a blizzard to complete his leg of the journey. Knight's heroic flight aroused public interest in airmail service and paved the way for such improvements as beacons, lighted runways and radio service. ■ While airmail was revolutionizing the skies, a quiet transformation was also taking place on the ground—the mechanization of commercial mail. Companies began purchasing and using— on their premises—approved meter machines that imprinted the proper postage, date and place of mailing. ■ Mechanized processing equipment was also being tried in post offices. Amazingly similar to the letter sorting machines that would come in the 1960s, the "mail distributing and assembling apparatus" tested in Chicago and the "automatic multiple-distributer" tested in Washington, DC, were capable of sorting letters to 120 separations. Despite their obvious potential, the machines were not approved for national use. ■ In another time, ideas like mechanized mail processing might have been readily accepted. But in 1929, the Great Depression changed what had been a period of prosperity to one of ultimate despair. No aspect of American life would remain untouched—including the postal system.

Starting Propeller.

Above: *Early airmail pilot signaling assistants to give the propeller a spin. U.S. Air Mail Service instructions were explicit on handling problem takeoffs: "In case the engine fails at takeoff, land straight ahead regardless of obstacles."*

Above: *President Wilson (left) and Major R.H. Fleet, in charge of airmail operations, shown here before the first regularly scheduled airmail flight in 1918. From Washington's Potomac Park, pilot Lt. George Boyle was scheduled to fly to Philadelphia, 128 miles away. But, once airborne, the young pilot encountered problems with the in-flight compass of his Curtiss Jenny biplane and crash-landed near Waldorf, Maryland, only 20 miles from Washington and in the opposite direction from Philadelphia. Boyle was not seriously injured.*

Left: Lieutenant James C. Edgerton was presented with roses by his sister Elizabeth after completing the last leg of the airmail flight on May 15, 1918, from Philadelphia to Washington. Edgerton flew the final leg of the first regularly scheduled airmail route from Washington to Philadelphia to New York and back. In his 52 airmail flights, Edgerton had only one forced landing.

Above: Country postmasters, such as Notch, Missouri's Levi ("Uncle

Ike") Morrill, shown here in 1926, were often well-known local citizens.

Morrill, over 90 in this photograph, was Notch Postmaster for 32 years.

Left: Post offices have long been a focal point for the community,

as shown by this gathering of Boy Scouts outside the Oak Park, Illinois,

Post Office in the 1920s.

Above: While an armed guard stands by, mail is unloaded from National Air Transport plane at Cleveland in 1928. **Left:** Deserting his desk in the Chicago, Illinois Federal Building, Postmaster Arthur C. Leuder garbed himself in a regulation mail carrier's uniform, borrowed a mail pouch from one of his men, and personally delivered the first Christmas Sealed letter opening the 1925 campaign to raise funds to fight tuberculosis.

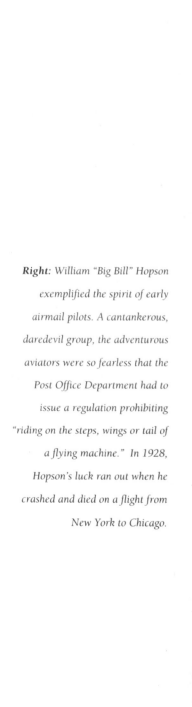

Right: William "Big Bill" Hopson
exemplified the spirit of early
airmail pilots. A cantankerous,
daredevil group, the adventurous
aviators were so fearless that the
Post Office Department had to
issue a regulation prohibiting
"riding on the steps, wings or tail of
a flying machine." In 1928,
Hopson's luck ran out when he
crashed and died on a flight from
New York to Chicago.

Above: By the time she retired from the Washington, DC, Mail Equipment Shop in 1923, Carrie L. Hurley had sewn 48 million mailbag seams. She performed the same job for 26 years.

Above: *Though Hawaii would not become a state for 59 years, the United States Post Office Department incorporated the Hawaiian postal system in 1900.*

Left: *Relying on natural formations as landmarks, mail-carrying contractor F.E. Stevens is pictured in 1920 carrying an 80-pound mail pack on skis through the mountain passes from Rocky Bar to Atlanta, Idaho. During avalanche season, carriers traveled in pairs— a quarter-mile apart—in case of an emergency.*

Above: Mail orders requesting tickets for the 1929 World Series came to Philadelphia's Shibe Park by the truckload. Hometown fans fortunate enough to purchase seats were, no doubt, delighted with the results. Philadelphia swept the series against Chicago, four games to one.
Right: Louisville, Kentucky's Post Office staged this whimsical 1927 photograph of Santa and two armed guards transporting "wish letters" from that city's children. Post offices had been accepting letters addressed to Santa Claus since 1912. "Responsible persons" were permitted to review the correspondence and send Christmas gifts to young writers.

Above: *Before earning worldwide acclaim, Charles Lindbergh carried airmail between St. Louis and Chicago as a pilot for the Robertson Aircraft Corporation. In 1927, following his return from Paris after the historic transatlantic flight, he noted: "All Europe looks on U.S. airmail service with reverence. There is nothing like it anywhere abroad."*

Above: In a 1925 flight from Chicago to Cleveland, Wesley L. Smith's plane caught fire and began a vertical drop. Through a series of skillful maneuvers, Smith regained navigational control and landed in a cornfield without injury to himself, his co-pilot, or the U.S. Mail.

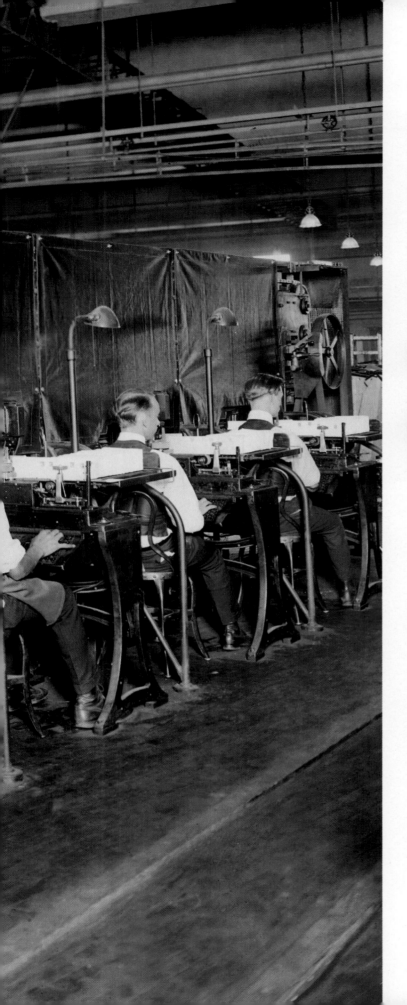

Above: *Following World War I, the Post Office Department converted Army trucks to Parcel Post vehicles. In this 1919 photograph, the yield of a New England oyster bed is being placed in the truck for transport to a nearby public school.* **Left:** *The Gehring Mail Distributing Machine was briefly tested by the Washington, DC, Post Office beginning in 1922. Five clerks sitting at keyboards could sort mail to 120 separations, twice the number possible with a manual sorting case. Though the machine showed promise, mail processing technology advanced little during the following decades. Americans had other concerns: the Great Depression and World War II. Not until the 1950s would a viable, nonmanual sorting system become reality.*

"The Night Mail"

Above: Early airmail landing strips were usually nothing more than rural fields. Equipment was equally poor. Planes had no instrument panels, and one navigational tool was a partially filled bottle rigged as a level indicator. In the government operation of airmail service from 1918 to 1927, 43 persons lost their lives, including 32 pilots. Over 6,500 flights were forced down due to hazardous weather conditions. *Left:* By 1929, moving the mail at night had become routine. Early airmail pilots flying at night had no radar, fancy instrumentation or air traffic controllers to help guide their way. Instead, they relied on a network of revolving beacons mounted on 50-foot towers. Serving as "airplane lighthouses," the beacons revolved three times per minute and could be seen for more than 100 miles.

Above: "Wrap securely, address plainly and mail early" was the suggestion of post offices in 1920 to customers mailing Christmas parcels. Even today, the "Mail Early" campaign remains a part of the holiday postal program. *Left:* In this 1917 photograph, a Lake Minnetonka, Minnesota, Parcel Post carrier provides service in addition to delivering mail. Here, the carrier weighs a child as part of a public health program to extend medical services to rural areas. In summer, mail trucks also brought farm produce to customers as part of regular rural free delivery (RFD) service. RFD service also moved entire tobacco crops in Kentucky, fruit in Florida and California, and celery in Colorado.

Above: In 1923, 51 thoroughbreds valued at $1 million were shipped from France to the United States and unloaded in specially crafted U.S. Mail cargo crates. **Left:** Armed guards and even U.S. Marines escorted some postal vehicles along city streets in the 1920s. Following the Federal Reserve's decision to ship currency by mail, nearly $20 million was stolen in a six-year crime spree that plagued the Post Office Department. Railway clerks armed with automatic handguns and sawed-off shotguns were authorized to "kill or disable any person engaged in the theft or robbery" of the mails.

Above: *In 1926 Genevieve Baskfield of Zumbrota, Minnesota, was a carrier in the Village Delivery Service, which served communities that received neither city nor rural mail service. Village Delivery was discontinued in 1971, but the role of women in the postal system continued to grow.*

Above: *In the early days of airmail, postal employees transferred mailbags from truck to plane, while the pilot, sitting in the cramped cockpit, anxiously prepared for takeoff. Biplanes such as the de Havilland 4 generally carried 100–500 pounds of mail on flights of 350 miles or less.*

Above: In 1926, the Post Office Department awarded the first contract airmail (CAM) routes to commercial airline companies. In this photograph, passengers aboard one of the CAM 9 flights from Chicago to Minneapolis pose during a stop in Milwaukee. Northwest Airlines was awarded the CAM 9 route after the previous contractor failed to reach Minneapolis four out of six flights. Ironically, the inaugural Northwest flight also failed to reach its destination, crashing on takeoff.

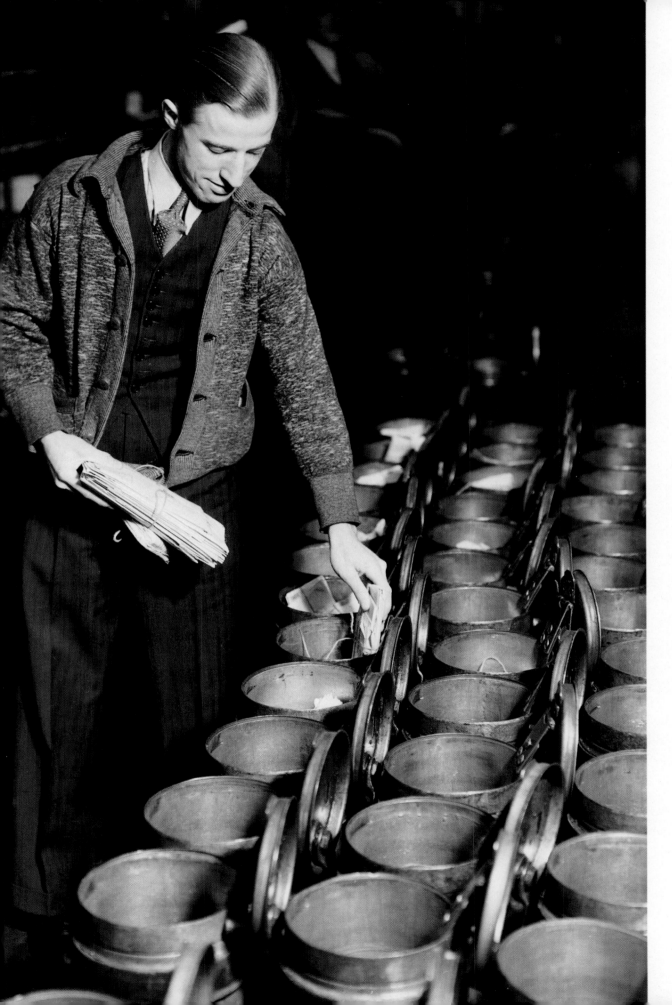

Left: *In the 1920s, the New York City Post Office relied on an intricate 27-mile underground pneumatic tube system to send mail to branches and stations. Each tube held 600 letters which traveled at the rate of 30 miles per hour. Pneumatic tubes were used intermittently from 1893–1953 in a number of large cities.*

1931-1945

Silent Heroics in Troubled Times

Throughout the 1930s, the Great Depression left its mark. More than 17 million people lost their livelihoods. Businesses closed. Over 5,000 banks failed. Industry came to a halt. Farm prices hit rock bottom. Families lost their homes and were forced to endure the indignity of standing in government soup lines. Only through the spirited new ideas and leadership of President Franklin D. Roosevelt did the nation recover from the dismal situation. ■ Roosevelt's choice to lead the Post Office Department during these lean years was James A. Farley, and he led with authority. Despite a failing American economy, Farley's Department showed a surplus six out of nine years. He inaugurated transatlantic and transpacific airmail, established the 40-hour work week and opened hundreds of new post offices around the country. ■ By 1940, when Farley left as Postmaster General, the Depression had waned, but post offices and the American public faced a new challenge—the threat of war. As Americans geared up for possible involvement, the postal system played its part. Mail trucks displayed placards promoting national defense. Post offices performed many of the same nonpostal services provided during World War I. And, when the United States entered the war in 1941, thousands of postal employees enlisted for armed service. ■ War shortages in staff and equipment posed unique challenges for post offices. One particularly troubling problem was the deterioration of the postal fleet. Model A wooden-sided trucks—already in use for nearly 15 years—were greatly in need of repair or replacement, but no new

postal vehicles were available. Even if they had been, gasoline rationing would have limited their use. As a result, many carriers utilized public transportation for the duration of the war. ■ Once again, as in World War I, women filled the gap caused by the movement of skilled male postal workers to military service. By 1944, 18,000 postmasters, 13,000 clerks, 229 city carriers and 770 rural carriers were female. ■ Getting the tremendous volume of mail to GIs stationed overseas required special planning. To save precious space on transport ships and planes, the government developed the V-Mail system of photographing letters. Each letter was photographed on 16 mm film along with 1,800 others. When the rolls of film reached their destination, each letter was reproduced onto 4-by-3¼-inch photos and delivered to the addressee. ■ One sack of V-Mail weighed 45 pounds and contained 150,000 letters versus 2,575 pounds and 37 sacks needed for ordinary mail. Between 1942 and 1945, U.S. Service personnel sent and received 233 million V-Mail letters. ■ The dedication of postal employees during World War II was not overlooked. In his 1945 report to Congress, Postmaster General Robert Hannegan directed "honor and gratitude on the 56,140 postal personnel" who had served their country during the war. Americans and the Post Office Department would now set about rebuilding the country. "Now more than ever," noted Hannegan, "the Post Office Department must be responsive to the people's will and do its part in bringing to all the blessings of peace and prosperity."

Above: *In addition to the mammoth task of handling mail for servicemen during World War II in conjunction with the War and Navy Departments, the Post Office was given many nonpostal responsibilities, including the registration of aliens and the sale of bonds to finance the war effort. Here, a Minnesota postmaster displays his patriotic "Defense Window" in 1942.*

Above: Shawneetown, Illinois, 1937. Despite pay furloughs, the Post Office was a solid source of employment during the Great Depression, providing a steady income for those lucky enough to hold or land postal jobs. **Right:** The Sprott, Alabama, Post Office, photographed by Walker Evans in 1936, doubled as a general store. Many smaller rural post offices have traditionally been located in the postmaster's home or place of business.

Above: Postmaster General James A. Farley, an avid airmail supporter, is surrounded by thousands of cards, letters and packages mailed to him during National Air Mail Week. The massive promotion, launched during the week of May 15–21, 1938, was organized to commemorate the 20th anniversary of scheduled airmail service and to educate the public about the progress and benefits of airmail service. Farley expressed his gratitude for the 150,000 pieces of mail in a national radio address several weeks later. *Right:* One of the Post Office Department's truly monumental innovations was the Railway Post Office (RPO). When the RPO was at its peak in the 1930s, more than 30,000 postal employees sorted mail aboard 4,000 moving trains. In this photograph, an RPO clerk operates an odd-looking contraption called a "catcher arm." With this peculiar device, workers could snatch outgoing mailbags hung on poles at train stations and avoid time-consuming stops.

Above: In 1935, in an underground igloo at the South Pole, postal employee Charles F. Anderson
canceled thousands of pieces of philatelic mail carried by Admiral Byrd's expedition to "Little America."
Byrd's service charge for transporting the postal covers on the 16,000-mile journey was 50 cents for each
piece of mail. *Left:* Post offices have long been community gathering places. Here, in the 1940s, three
residents of French Settlement, Louisiana, pass the time away on the front steps of the rustic post office.

Right: Combining the romance of riding the rails with the tradition of moving the mails, the Railway Post Office (RPO) was a true American icon. By the time this photograph was taken in 1945, however, the number of RPOs was undergoing a steady decline. This postal heritage eventually ended in 1977, when the Washington to New York RPO made its final run.

Left: *With her husband off fighting in World War II, Elsie Martin of Finleyville, Pennsylvania, took over the duties on his rural route. Thousands of women entered the postal work force as part of the war effort, and many continued working even after the battles had long ended.*

Above: When it opened in 1934, the Chicago Post Office became the largest postal facility in the world. *Left:* In the summer of 1940, some rural Kentucky carriers still relied on horse and carriage. Here, a rural carrier outside the town of Morehead transfers letters and parcels to another carrier's saddlebags. The horseback carrier then delivered the mail to residents of the hollows and hills, where wagons and automobiles could not pass. Horseback deliveries continued in Kentucky until the 1970s.

Above: Gathering the morning mail at 18 degrees below zero during February 1942 in Morton County, North Dakota.

Above: *Adobe and log post office in Costilla, New Mexico, 1940.*

Above: A New York Post Office employee loads a stamp-canceling machine in 1931. ***Right:*** *Mailboxes, such as this one in Omaha, Nebraska, in 1938, were not a common sight until the 1920s. Prior to that time letter carriers had to knock on doors, ring doorbells, or use whistles to alert the residents of mail delivery. If the occupant was not home, the carrier had to take the mail back to the post office and attempt delivery on the next trip.*

Above: *During World War II, the ingenious V-Mail program was instituted, combining the latest in microfilm technology with the age-old practice of letter-writing. Here, an American servicewoman holds one V-Mail pouch containing 80 film rolls carrying the 114,000 letters in the mailbags surrounding her.*

Left: *Mail call on the fighting fronts of World War II. Corporal Albert Franczaini of Kensington, Indiana, passes out mail to a group of soldiers ensconced in a French barn in 1944.*

Above: Rows of glistening steel mailboxes have long been a familiar landmark of rural America. In this 1942 photograph, Earl Axel Westerberg checks his mailbox on the way to work at Ford's River Rouge plant in Detroit. This style of box first appeared in 1915 and was designed by a postal employee, Roy Joroleman. **Right:** On occasions when Railway Post Office trains stopped at stations, the "catcher arm" gave way to manual loading methods, as in this 1940 photograph by Arthur Rothstein taken in Carson City, Nevada.

1946-1970

Gizmos and Gadgets Galore

To American GIs returning home after World War II, the future seemed full of promise. Changes in the postal system reflected these heady times. ■ New technologies devised during the war were quickly becoming part of American life, and postal managers wanted to exploit them. For better or worse, a number of mechanical gizmos and gadgets, such as rocket mail, speedmail, the Mailster and Mailomat, made their way into the mail system. Some, like rocket mail and the autogyro—half plane and half helicopter—were utter failures. Others, like the Transorma letter sorter, laid the groundwork for advances in postal operations that came later. ■ This tinkering with traditional postal methods started in 1946, when helicopter mail service was begun in several large cities, including Chicago. The helicopters could leapfrog traffic jams on the ground, and they cut the time needed to move mail from Chicago's Midway Airport to the post office from 90 minutes to just 15. By the 1950s the Chicago Post Office had seven helicopters carrying mail to and from 52 post offices in 32 suburban communities. Post offices also looked into new ways of moving mail on the ground with the three-wheeled Mailster and the compact Jeep. As types of delivery vehicles multiplied, the Post Office in 1954 also changed its colors, from the traditional olive drab to today's red, white and blue. ■ The vehicle and color changes, however, were not nearly as significant as changes made in mail processing during this time. By the 1950s with annual mail volume at 50 billion pieces and climbing, it had become obvious that people sorting mail by hand couldn't handle the ever-growing mail stream. New mail handling equipment and methods had to be developed, and they were. ■ By the 1960s, mechanized letter sorting machines (LSMs) had come into wide use. The introduction in 1963 of the Zone Improvement Plan (ZIP) Code was crucial to making the new equipment work by enabling LSM clerks to sort mail to the right destination. Postal workers could process and deliver ZIP-Coded mail up to 24 hours faster than mail without the codes. ■ Along with ZIP Codes, the Post Office introduced other new services and processing changes such as simplified postmarks, Priority Mail, MAILGRAM and an innovative experimental service called Express Mail. ■ While improvements in mail processing and transporting came thick and fast during this period, postal employees' pay stayed pretty much the same. By 1964, the average postal worker was unhappily making only $5,000 to $6,000 a year—less than a New York City sanitation worker. ■ Other problems faced the Post Office Department, too: Local post offices were outdated and overcrowded; postmasters' jobs were still being filled by political patronage; and postal managers faced restrictive laws every time they tried to make a decision. At a 1967 congressional oversight hearing, Postmaster General Lawrence O'Brien made a case for postal reform so he and postal managers could have more control over workload, rates, revenues, facilities, work conditions and transportation. ■ Clearly, conditions were ripe for change. It would come in 1971.

Right: Three-wheeled Mailsters, also called "Scooters," were used by many carriers on their routes from the mid-1950s until the early 1970s.

Above: *After World War II, the Post Office Department contracted with several airlines to test mail sorting in flight aboard transcontinental "flying post offices" such as "Midnight Expediter" which flew between Los Angeles and Boston.* **Left:** *The bus version of the Railway Post Office (RPO) was the Highway Post Office (HPO), a common sight from 1941 to 1974. Workers aboard "Hypos" sorted mail en route, unlike regular Star Route vehicles which only transported mail. In 1960 there were over 200 HPO routes averaging about 150 miles each.*

Above: Over the years, many post offices have experimented with drive-through windows. Here, a customer drops off mail with a Houston, Texas, postal clerk. **Right:** An ocean of letter carriers parade down the steps of the main post office in New York City in 1967. During this period, ten percent of all mail nationwide was handled and delivered through this office.

Above: *Helicopters were used in Los Angeles for transporting the mail. Here, two men transfer the day's mail from an airplane to a helicopter that will deliver the precious cargo to the L.A. Post Office.*
Left: *January 28, 1955, spelled the end of an era for Philadelphia letter carrier Adolphe Lampe and his horse "Dusty." After that day, motorized vehicles would deliver the mail along the narrow streets of the City of Brotherly Love.*

Above: In 1963, to encourage the use of the new five digit ZIP (Zone Improvement Plan) Code for improved mail processing, Postmaster General J. Edward Day introduced "Mr. ZIP." Part of the nationwide promotional campaign included Mr. ZIP buttons and carrier satchels and the recruitment of Ethel Merman to sing the Disney tune "Zip-A-Dee-Doo-Dah" on public service broadcasts.

Left: With dexterity and precision, this employee of the Bureau of Engraving and Printing double-checks a press run of the 1947 stamps commemorating the 100th anniversary of the U.S. postage stamp. Even now, five decades later, quality control is still performed by a human being with an attentive eye.

Above: *The postman rings 119 times at this rural spot in the Fairmount Hills section of Syracuse, New York, where thoughtful residents strung their mailboxes in one long row to spare the postman's feet.* **Right:** *Despite advances in transportation technology, delivering the mail the old fashioned way was still in use in rural areas in 1955.*

Above: Mrs. Scott Young at work in the post office and general store in Matinicus Island, Maine, 1950.

Left: The lobby of Montgomery, Alabama's post office in 1956.

Above: City carrier Oscar Tanguay in Bath, Maine, in the early 1950s.

Right: Silver Spring, Maryland's "Transorma" automatic letter sorter signaled the dawn of the era of modern postal mechanization in 1957. Precursor of the modern letter sorting machine, the machine was operated by five keyboard operators capable of sorting 15,000 letters per hour to 300 possible destinations. Postmaster General Arthur E. Summerfield characterized the experimental machines as "a forward step of great significance for the American postal service."

Above: In 1949, the American-Canadian border ran straight through the center of the Norton, Vermont, Post Office. Customers actually entered from the United States but left the building into Canada.

Above: During the 1950s, Mobile, Alabama's letter carriers sequence

their mail by "pigeon hole."

Above: Three boxes of chirping baby chicks was the postal bounty for this Mississippi farmer one summer day in 1955. Rural carriers have delivered many live animals through the mails including quail, partridges, ducks, geese, and turkeys. **Right:** In the 1960s, five giant mailboxes in Manhattan and the Bronx helped handle Christmas season stamp sales.

125

Above: In 1947, Charles Dick served the customers of rural free delivery (RFD) Route 1 in northeast Virginia from his "post office on wheels." Rural carriers sold stamps, postal cards and envelopes; registered letters and money orders; delivered, weighed and accepted parcels; and even administered oaths to pensioners when completing their pay vouchers. Today, RFD carriers continue to provide a wide variety of such services. *Left:* During the 1960 Christmas season, after finding that 10,000 holiday mailings had insufficient postage, Minneapolis postal employees donated their own time and money to buy and post stamps on the envelopes.

Above: *In August of election year 1964, Postmaster General John A. Gronouski dedicated the "Register to Vote" stamp in Washington. The enlarged photograph of President Lyndon B. Johnson conspicuously placed behind the podium left no doubt about whom Mr. Gronouski supported for the upcoming election.*
Left: *A mail distribution clerk in 1946.*

1971–Today

"The U.S. Postal Service: We Deliver!"

The American postal system has seen more changes in the past 20 years than in the previous 200. The most sweeping change came in 1971, when the old Post Office Department became the United States Postal Service (USPS). This overhaul set up a Postal Board of Governors and took the Postmaster General out of the President's Cabinet. It freed postal managers from having elected officials looking over their shoulders every time they made a decision. It let them usher in more efficient methods. It empowered postal unions to bargain for their members over wages and working conditions. In these and other ways, it made the Postal Service independent. ■ One side of postal operations has not changed. Like its predecessor, the Postal Service gives efficient, dependable service to all U.S. residents, and at lower rates than people in other industrialized nations pay. Giving that level of service requires a huge commitment by postal workers. Six days a week, the 775,000 Postal Service employees process and deliver 650 million pieces of mail to more than 130 million addresses on 230,000 city and rural routes around the country. ■ The three decades since the 1971 postal overhaul have brought a lot of progress, notably in the area of mail processing. During the 1960s and 1970s, the focus was on having mechanized letter sorting machines handle an ever-rising share of the mail. But by the 1980s, the Postal Service had begun to automate its operations. Automated equipment still was processing less than 50 percent of all mail in 1991, but it soon would replace mechanical and manual sorting as the

dominant mail-processing method. More recent innovations such as remote barcoding have automated mail processing even more. ■ Customer-conscious postal workers have found their own ways to improve service and to make customers aware of it. In 1988 in High Point, North Carolina, letter carriers began backing up their promise of quality service by paying customers 25 cents for each piece of misdelivered mail. Not many quarters changed hands. ■ In the other 40,000 post offices around the country, employees also are living up to the organization's credo: "We Deliver." Service is getting better and the public knows it. Major surveys show the American public puts the Postal Service at the top in terms of service—even ahead of banks and phone companies. And innovation is now part of the Postal Service's internal culture, with new products and service features being tested on a regular basis. ■ From the tropics of American Samoa to Alaska's frozen tundra, from the barren flats of Death Valley to the skyscrapers of New York City, America's sprawling postal network is a vital link in allowing people in the U.S. to communicate better. ■ An inscription on the old City Post Office building (now the National Postal Museum) in Washington, DC, calls the postal system the "promoter of mutual acquaintance, of peace and goodwill among men and nations." In a time of ever-changing high technology, it's reassuring to know that the U.S. Postal Service still carries that noble tradition of service to a personal level in communities large and small. Ben Franklin would have been proud.

Above: In 1987, for the first time since the transcontinental airmail routes of the 1920s, the Postal Service contracted a fleet of aircraft exclusively to transport mail. Here, planes are loaded at the Terre Haute, Indiana airport, which acts as a hub for the Express and Priority Mail services.

Above: *New York City's General Post Office manual letter-sorting operation, 1972.*

Left: *On August 12, 1970, the Post Office Department became the United States Postal Service. As Postmaster General Winton Blount looked on, President Richard M. Nixon signed the postal reform bill into law during ceremonies attended by members of the Cabinet and Congress. The law transformed mail delivery from a political patronage operation into a modern self-sustaining business.*

Above: Boston clerk under sorting scheme, 1972. **Left:** During a postal career spanning

five decades, 78-year-old Moses Walters rode horse and mule more than 500,000 miles to

deliver mail to Appalachian residents near Stella, Kentucky. When he began in 1926,

Walters was paid a dime a day for the 40-mile, six-day-per-week route.

*Above: Before automation, there was mechanization with mail processing through the use of letter sorting machines (LSMs). Here, Merrifield, Virginia LSM clerks key in sorting codes while, **right,** another clerk empties the 120 bins behind her into trays for dispatch at the Chicago, Illinois facility.*

Above: Rural mailboxes near Bismarck, North Dakota, in 1976. **Left:** Processing the mail for local
and out-of-town delivery is an exacting, streamlined process. Every day in 40,000 post offices,
stations and branches around the country, workers cull and sort flats, parcels and letter mail
for delivery to American households and businesses. This 1976 photograph shows a typical day
on the workroom floor of the Washington, DC, Post Office.

Above: Tucked away on the ground floor of a majestic convent is the 30-by-12-foot
Nazareth, Michigan, Post Office, operated by Sister/Postmaster Marciana Hennig
shown here in 1977. Though the Postal Service paid her a salary for her duties,
Sister Mariana signed over the check to the convent community.
She was the fourth sister of St. Joseph to serve as postmaster since 1899.
Right: The Integrated Buffer System shown here in Fort Myers, Florida,
is an experimental system developed to help process large volumes of mail.
This unit holds an average of 55,000 letters at a time in its system.

Above: Chinatown Station in San Francisco in 1972. Station superintendent E. H. Lum assists one of the neighborhood's residents. **Right:** Mule train remains the most practical and reliable way to deliver mail to the Grand Canyon's Havasupai Indian reservation.

Above: First deployed in the early 1980s, bar code sorters such as this are now in wide use around the postal system. Following sorting by optical character readers, the bar code sorters make a secondary sort which translates into more consistent delivery and service to customers.

Left: Prior to mechanization and then automation, clerks memorized complicated mail processing schemes in order to sort letters down to the local carrier route. Despite constantly improving technologies, mail still must be sorted by hand at a letter carrier's work station prior to delivery.

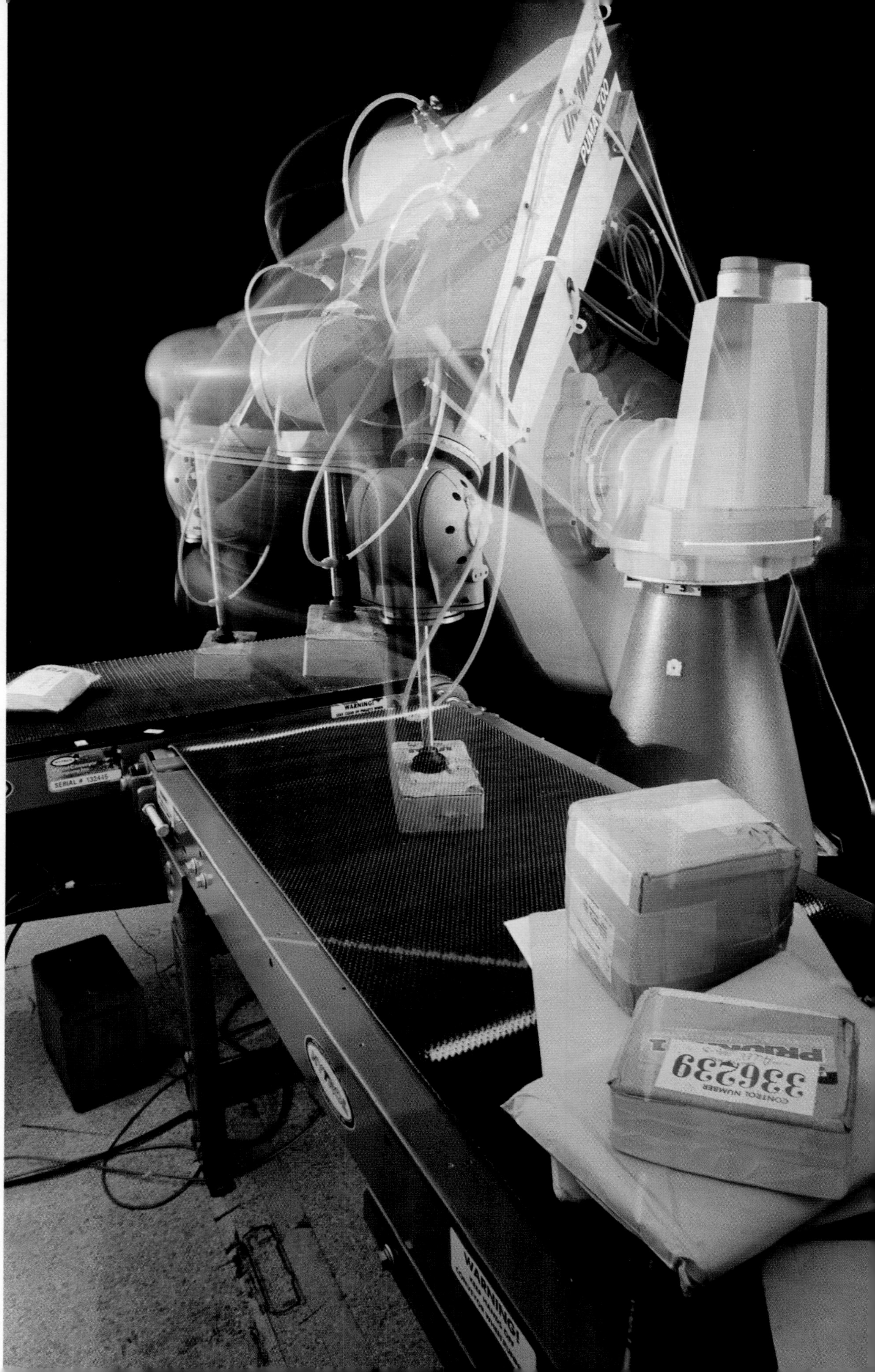
SERIAL # 132445
CONTROL NUMBER
336239

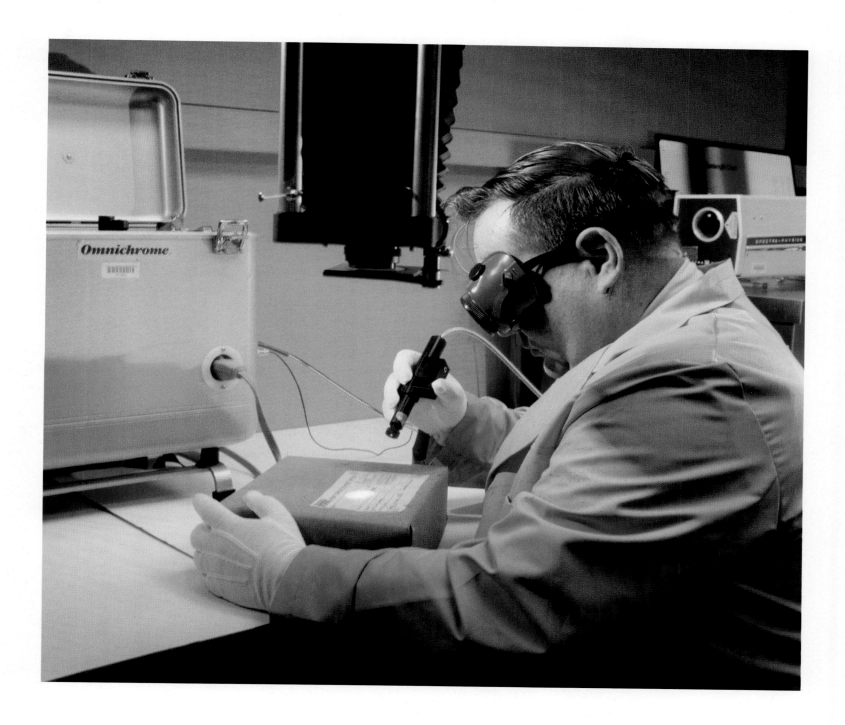

147

Left: The Postal Service uses experimental robotics equipment to research methods of handling the mail faster, less expensively, and more efficiently. **Above:** A forensic analyst in the Postal Service Inspection Service Crime Lab in Washington, D.C. uses laser technology to search for latent fingerprints on a package which was involved in a criminal case.

Above: Postmistress Evelyn Shealy lowers the flag at the close of a day's business
at the nation's smallest post office building, a converted fertilizer shed that is 7 feet,
3 inches wide, 8 feet, 4 inches deep and 10 feet, 6 inches high. In the heart of the
Florida Everglades, the Ochopee post office opened "temporarily" in 1953 after
the general store it was housed in burned. *Left:* A mail handler at work in 1973
at the Philadelphia Post Office loading dock.

Above: Of the 612 families on Levi U. Fisher's Gap, Pennsylvania, route, more than half were Amish, many with the same first and last name. Fisher was believed to be the only Amish carrier in America at the time of this photograph. **Left:** *Letter carrier Robert W. Miller, Coal City, Illinois, 1973. The Coal City Post Office started using bicycles in 1949.*

Above: Because of their sheer enormity, Bulk Mail Centers (BMCs), like this one in Capitol Heights, Maryland, use trained technicians to monitor processing operations via an intricate system of cameras. **Right:** Kearney, New Jersey employees sort parcels in 1973. Large facilities like this one are strategically located around the country to efficiently handle the nation's package volume.

Above: Seven days a week, 365 days a year, in communities large and small,
and in all kinds of weather, postal employees collect letters, flats and parcels and
send them on to their destination. Here, a carrier in Falls Church, Virginia,
removes mail from a collection box during a 1975 snowstorm. **Left:** In tiny, isolated
Alaskan outposts like Rampart, mail and other necessities of life arrive by snowmobile.
Daniel Weihl is shown here unloading mail, including parcels containing butter,
crackers, canned meat, cookies and warm clothing.

Above: Letter carriers such as this one in New York City delivered nearly 69 million pieces of Express Mail in 1999 alone. *Left:* Mail handlers on a curling line in Merrifield, Virginia, in 1977 pull out odd-sized pieces of mail for separate processing.

Above: A letter carrier in Washington, DC in 1973. Letter carriers deliver the mail on approximately 200,000 rural and city routes to over 116 million addresses each business day. *Left:* No snow is too deep, no conditions too harsh, to keep this carrier and his canine companion from completing their daily delivery route. In this 1971 photograph, you can almost feel the peaceful tranquility of the moment.

Above: *Rural letter carrier near Cleveland, Ohio, 1975.*

Right: *Rural carrier Norm Little, Bismarck, North Dakota, 1976.*

Above: In the early 1980s, the Postal Service began wide use of automation. Optical character readers, such as the one shown here in Los Angeles, can "read" and sort 30,000 pieces of mail per hour. *Left:* More than 650 million pieces of mail are delivered each day by postal employees, including parcels of every shape and size. Here a Bulk Mail Center employee deals with the thousands of parcels to be processed that day.

Above: Similar to bar code scanners at grocery store checkouts, the optical character reader (OCR) is the key for the Postal Service's plan to completely automate mail processing by being capable of sorting 30,000 letters per hour. *Left:* Junius Faulk proudly displays his tractor trailer and its stylized advertisement for Express Mail in Merrifield, Virginia, in 1985. Today, a postal fleet of some 180,000 vehicles traverses the nation's highways in an effort to deliver excellence for less.

Postal Stamps

The stamps and stationery items depicted here, and on the next three pages, feature subjects relating to the Postal Service and its employees.

2¢ Post Rider
Issued March 27, 1869

10¢ Messenger Running
Issued October 1, 1885

10¢ Messenger Running
Issued January 24, 1893

10¢ Messenger Running
Issued October 10, 1894

10¢ Messenger on Bicycle
Issued December 9, 1902

3¢ Railway Postal Clerk
Issued April 5, 1913

2¢ City Carrier
Issued July 1, 1913

1¢ Post Office Clerk
Issued July 1, 1913

4¢ Rural Carrier
Issued July 1, 1913

5¢ Mail Train
Issued July 1, 1913

10¢ Steamship and Mail Tender
Issued July 1, 1913

15¢ Automobile Service
Issued July 1, 1913

20¢ Aeroplane Carrying Mail
Issued July 1, 1913

10¢ Postman & Motorcycle
Issued July 12, 1922

15¢ Postman & Motorcycle
Issued April 25, 1925

20¢ Post Office Truck
Issued April 25, 1925

3¢ Pony Express
Issued April 9, 1940

17¢ Postman & Motorcycle
Issued October 30, 1944

10¢ Post Office Department
Building
Issued November 18, 1949

20¢ Delivery of Letter
Issued October 13, 1954

15¢ Letter Carrier
Issued June 6, 1955

30¢ Delivery of Letter
Issued September 3, 1957

4¢ Overland Mail
Issued October 10, 1958

4¢ Pony Express
Issued July 19, 1960

4¢ Pony Express Rider
Envelope
Issued July 19, 1960

4¢ First Automated Post Office
Issued October 20, 1960

15¢ Montgomery Blair
Issued May 3, 1963

5¢ City Mail Delivery
Issued October 26, 1963

10¢ 50th Anniversary U.S. Mail Service
Issued May 15, 1968

8¢ U.S. Postal Service
Issued July 1, 1971

8¢ Postal Employees, Issued April 30, 1973

10¢ ZIP Code
Issued January 4, 1974

10¢ 200 Years of
Postal Service
Issued September 3,
1975

13¢ Old Post Office
St. Louis, Missouri
Postal Card
Issued October 14, 1982

13¢ Old Post Office
Washington, DC
Postal Card
Issued April 19, 1983

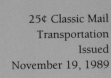

25¢ Letter Carriers
Issued August 30, 1989

25¢ Classic Mail
Transportation
Issued
November 19, 1989

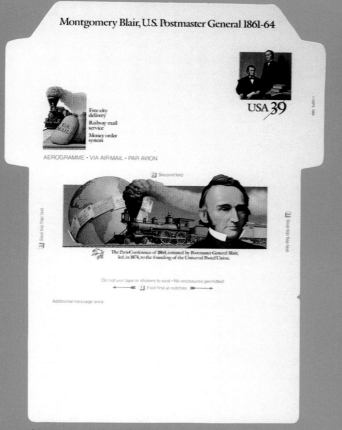

39¢ Montgomery Blair Aerogramme
Issued November 20, 1989

45¢ Future Mail Transportation
Issued November 28, 1989

$1 USPS/Olympic Rings
Issued
September 29, 1991

29¢ National Postal Museum
Issued July 30, 1993

32¢ Rural Free Delivery
Issued August 7, 1996

32¢ Stagecoach—Pacific 97
Issued March 13, 1997

32¢ Ship—Pacific 97
Issued March 13, 1997

Acknowledgments

Front Cover: ©New York City Public Library. **Page iv:** Grant Smith/Corbis-Bettmann. **Page 3:** ©U.S. Postal Service, John Garvey, photographer. **Page 5:** ©U.S. Postal Service. **Page 7:** ©U.S. Postal Service. **Pages 8 & 9:** Library of Congress, Matthew Brady Collection. **Page 10:** ©Milwaukee County Historical Society. **Page 11:** Library of Congress. **Page 12:** ©Oklahoma Historical Society. **Page 13:** Library of Congress. **Page 14:** ©Cedar Falls Historical Society. **Page 15:** ©Cincinnati Historical Society. **Page 16:** Smithsonian Institution. **Page 17:** ©Marion County, Oregon Historical Society photo 85.63.11. **Page 18:** ©Brown Brothers. **Page 19:** ©U.S. Postal Service. **Page 20:** ©Minnesota Historical Society. **Page 21:** Courtesy George Eastman House. **Page 22:** Library of Congress, Matthew Brady, photographer. **Page: 23:** ©State Historical Society of Wisconsin. **Pages 24 & 25:** ©U.S. Postal Service. **Page 26:** Chicago Historical Society. **Page 27:** Courtesy of the Cascade County Historical Society. **Page 29:** Photo by H.S. Poley, the Denver Public Library, Western History Collection. **Page 30:** ©U.S. Postal Service. **Page 31:** ©Culver Pictures, Inc. **Page 32:** ©Brown Brothers. **Pages 33 & 34:** ©U.S. Postal Service. **Page 35:** ©Evanston Historical Society. **Page 36:** ©Brown Brothers. **Page 37:** Carnegie Branch Library for Local History, Boulder Historical Society Collection. **Page 38:** ©U.S. Postal Service. **Page 39:** Library of Congress. **Pages 40-42:** ©U.S.

Postal Service. **Page 43:** Smithsonian Institution. **Page 44:** ©Whatcom Museum. **Page 45:** A. J. Bucks/National Archives. **Pages 46 & 47:** ©U.S. Postal Service. **Page 48:** Library of Congress. **Page 49:** ©U.S. Postal Service. **Page 50:** ©Kevin T. Farrell Collection. **Page 51:** ©Minnesota Historical Society. **Page 52:** Library of Congress. **Page 53:** National Archives. **Page 54:** ©U.S. Postal Service. **Page 55:** ©Historic Society of Delaware. **Page 56:** National Archives. **Page 57:** New York City Public Library. **Page 59:** ©U.S. Postal Service. **Page 60:** National Archives. **Page 61:** ©Corbis-Bettmann. **Page 62:** Library of Congress. **Page 63:** ©U.S. Postal Service. **Page 64:** Corbis/Underwood & Underwood. **Page 65:** Baldwin H. Wand/Corbis-Bettmann. **Page 66:** National Archives. **Page 67:** ©Corbis-Bettmann. **Page 68:** ©Bishop Museum, R. J. Baker Collection. **Page 69:** ©U.S. Postal Service. **Page 70:** ©Corbis-Bettmann. **Page 71:** ©University of Louisville Library, R. G. Patterson Collection. **Page 72:** ©Missouri Historical Society. **Pages 73 & 74:** ©U.S. Postal Service. **Page 75:** Underwood & Underwood/©Corbis-Bettmann. **Page 76:** Library of Congress, Fred Reed, photographer. **Page 77:** National Archives. **Page 78:** ©Minneapolis Public Library, Minneapolis Collection. **Pages 79 & 80:** ©Underwood & Underwood/Corbis-Bettmann. **Page 81:** ©Underwood & Underwood. **Page 82:** ©New York City Public Library. **Pages 83 & 84:** ©U.S. Postal Service. **Page 85:**

©Corbis-Bettmann. **Page 87**: Library of Congress, Jack DeLano, photographer. **Page 88**: Library of Congress, Russell Lee, photographer. **Page 89**: Library of Congress, Walker Evans, photographer. **Pages 90 & 91**: ©U.S. Postal Service. **Page 92**: The Historic New Orleans Collection, accession no. 1976.139.112. **Pages 93 & 94**: ©U.S. Postal Service. **Page 95**: ©UPI/Corbis-Bettmann. **Page 96**: Library of Congress, Marion Post Wolcott, photographer. **Page 97**: ©U.S. Postal Service. **Page 98**: Library of Congress, John Vachon, photographer. **Page 99**: Library of Congress, Russell Lee, photographer. **Page 100**: ©Corbis-Bettmann. **Page 101**: Library of Congress, John Vachon, photographer. **Pages 102 & 103**: National Archives. **Pages 104 & 105**: Library of Congress, Arthur Rothstein, photographer. **Pages 107-110**: ©U.S. Postal Service. **Page 111**: ©U.S. Postal Service, Atsuhiko (Sam) Tsunoda, photographer. **Page 112**: Temple University Libraries Photojournalism Collection. **Pages 113-115**: ©U.S. Postal Service. **Page 116**: ©UPI/Corbis-Bettmann. **Page 117**: ©Tony Stone Images. **Pages 118-120**: National Archives. **Page 121**: Library of Congress, U.S. News & World Report Collection, Warren K. Leffler, photographer. **Pages 122-124**: National Archives. **Page 125**: ©Library of Congress, New York World Telegram & Sun Collection. **Page 126**: National Archives. **Page 127**: ©University of Louisville Library, Standard Oil of NJ Collection, Libsohn, photographer. **Pages 128 & 129**: ©U.S. Postal Service, Frank

Alexander photographer. **Page 131**: ©U.S. Postal Service, Co Rentmeester, photographer. **Page 132**: National Archives. **Pages 133-140**: ©U.S. Postal Service, Patrick McCabe, photographer. **Page 141**: ©U.S. Postal Service, Gerald Merna, photographer. **Page 142**: ©U.S. Postal Service, Atsuhiko (Sam) Tsunoda, photographer. **Page 143**: ©U.S. Postal Service, Robert Martel, photographer. **Pages 144 & 145**: ©U.S. Postal Service, Patrick S. McCabe, photographer. **Page 146**: ©U.S. Postal Service. **Page 147**: ©U.S. Postal Service, Gerald Merna, photographer. **Page 148**: ©U.S. Postal Service, Patrick McCabe, photographer. **Page 149**: ©UPI/Corbis-Bettmann. **Pages 150-156**: ©U.S. Postal Service, Patrick McCabe, photographer. **Page 157**: ©U.S. Postal Service, Gerald Merna, photographer. **Page 158**: ©The Image Bank, Douglas Kirkland, photographer. **Page 159**: ©U.S. Postal Service, Patrick McCabe, photographer. **Page 160**: ©U.S. Postal Service, Richard Smolko, photographer. **Pages 161-165**: ©U.S. Postal Service, Patrick McCabe, photographer. **Page 171**: Library of Congress, Arthur Rothstein, photographer. **Page 172**: ©U.S. Postal Service, Gerald Merna, photographer. **Back Cover**: UT Institute of Texan Culture at San Antonio, ©The San Antonio Light Collection. **All stamps**: ©U.S. Postal Service.

Above: Adjacent to the Capitol building, the former Washington DC Post Office now serves as repository for the nation's postal heritage as the National Postal Museum.

Above: *The Postal Service workforce—more than 800,000*

strong—delivers to Americans every day, everywhere,

through rain, sleet and snow.